THE CHOICE IS REAL

The Choice Is Real
© 2023 Jayson Keery

ISBN 978-1-988355-34-4
All rights reserved

Published by Metatron Press
Montreal, Quebec
www.metatron.press

Printed in Canada
First printing

Editor | Hannah Karpinski
Cover photo | Antonia Colodro

Library and Archives Canada Cataloguing in Publication
Title: The choice is real / Jayson Keery.
Names: Keery, Jayson, author.
Description: Poems.
Identifiers: Canadiana 20230145299 | ISBN 9781988355344 (softcover)
Classification: LCC PS3611.E3757 C56 2023 | DDC 811/.6—dc23

THE
CHOICE
IS REAL

JAYSON KEERY

Metatron Press

THE CHOICE IS REAL

THE CHOICE IS REAL

*I love being
a girl. So delicate.*

- Lou Sullivan

Dedicated to those forced to prove it.

THE CHOICE IS REAL

I wake up most mornings
to do what.
Dress my genitals for
occasion. What odd
formality. What
choices. A
twat cravat. A
Hanes which way.
Fruit of the looming
cunt cataclysm.
Will I bite.
I wake up
to find I am
asked to stand. Like
brothers and sisters.
Will you.
The scroll of psychic
advertisements has
pinpointed my ambiguous
organs. I'm a match. Struck
and drafted into a
flaccid flame
brigade of
neutered fashion.
Keep it boxed and brief,
boring means boring into
the Man. We've got work to do

being normal and all, given
birth with no receipt,
this way. This certain way.
As if we had no choice.
As if we had no bodies to
move from. As if children
had no bodies. To move
from dream to cloud to
the rain somehow real
against my window.
I can stand it, the thought
of her here with me. Baby,
I know she wants to show.
Something of a tender
thong song drifting
to completion.

TANGLED THE RIBBON OF MY FAVORITE VHS...

How many wonders
    can one What
would I give if I could
    What the people know
I'm ready to know
    What a fire is
and why Live out
    these waters
that world
    This cavern
holds everything But
    is not
that world
    The girl who has
everything Answers

AND FELL THROUGH THE DARK

You can't protect children.
They know everything.
                    - Maurice Sendak

Out of her clothes and past the moon.

Stars like sugar on which her skin

feeds a distended corpse kneading

through black holes bloating along

the whole milked way. A feral yeast,

a starter starting and not stopping

through stars that never ask her to take mold.

They chatter through infinite constellations,

conversation, conversation.

She would be happy to do this—

float this out to infinity, if not

for the fucking sun, that virile sun,

making moon take shape,

a closed loop, a first poem, and her,

fat curdling against the sun's gaze,

light-spanked to a soft skin crust,

scrape it stir it make it.

She cries down from the heavens

I'm not the milk and the milk is not me.

But the earthlings are offended by her

child nudity, as if children

have no bodies. As if

children have no bodies,

no fears they need reflected,

a glass for looking no touch

went sourdough her nightmares

start to spill

THINGS I HAVE TIME

for Diane

to ask you who
to ask me if I love you how I could
how can family be
you're a step away from origin and not quite chosen by
me I was in love with your daughter is all
astrological opposites create a repulsive balance she was born
six months away from me my father born
six months away from you exactly repulsion I
told him to start dating you so I could get close
to your daughter
Whom do you love?

I'll ask later when it's easy
when you're up there looking down on earth
on your garden one of your many stages
of control what's control look like from way   up   there?
will you remember when I dragged a tree for you
full grown because who wants to wait
for children "hurry up!" I left a trail of slimed dirt
roiled the grass you raged "I'm gonna shoot you!"
when a shoe fell on a single living leaf of shrubbery
What does control look like from way up there?

I'm curious does the word begin mean anything
Now?

I imagine every time you wake up to begin a day
to begin and maybe end a day
you start by hitting a pool of breath a
cold surprise how cold a surprise
doesn't every surprise contain fear and a sickening joy?
Happy birthday.

To ask you of dismemberment feels so cruel
considering maybe I would ask
considering the time you told me not to
talk about my mastectomy at the dinner table because
some people don't have a choice
What does control look like from way up   there?

I think you were somehow born where I was born
but I never knew never thought to ask
still don't know still won't ask I don't
ask questions about my birth either maybe
there's something gay about this maybe
how much of this can I say is just that
Oops I'm transsexual and I can't text back.

This question is what made me think of you
made me laugh about when you once
handed me a copy of *Motherless Daughters*
which you had kickin' around because your mother
shot herself in the head in front of you I think I
never asked details or if I did it's not the kind of thing you
ask about twice I whispered "But my mother is still alive"
but my mother she was still alive

in fact she lived very much alive right down the long street
the author's first name is Hope the chapters I
remember, "When a Woman Needs a Woman: Gender Matters"
and "Daddy's Little Girl," which you always seemed angry about
saying he got between us saying I need a mother
we need a mother and Daddy needs a girl
Who hurt her?

What does it mean to exist in a shape now
for years your whole life you anguished
shape don't we women all try to take up less and
now what
how does it feel to eat
does it all feel so worthless
Now?

And this my biggest fear
the consequences already cropping up
my silence towards you does not go unnoticed
he said "Her dying wish to be close to her five children and
of the five you're the one outlier" yeah
what's so different about me what's so
different what's so different about me
just say it what's so different Daddy
I'm *your* little girl I'm here for you
except for when I'm not
except when I'm sneaking off
from the living funeral early
stole booze on the way out
Happy deathday.

How *are* you preparing for death?
What would you say
can you just say it
I know I can just say this to you.

But I won't and I think that's okay.

...ATTEMPT THE UNTANGLE...

You
    are the song I am
singing Steady boy
    steady
From sea to
    shining I am
awaiting Waiting
    forever to be
Together we come
    Under what sun
This is your world
    The boat is nearer
now I think
    I hear
her Awaiting
    your orders
World Your orders
    The land and the sea
1989
    Drummers
start drumming
    Trumpeters ready
A child born
    of sea and shore
Not ever before
    La-da-di-da
Up to the world of skies
    ...

TONIGHT I'M A PROBLEM

I shave

one leg

to feel

I am sleeping

with a woman

who is me

?

RUN, JENNY, RUN

Because you're tired
    of fight, freeze and fawning
over simple men
    who can't help
but get their way
    a starlit
a forest of forgiveness
    their way a creek
with too many paddles
    and he chose
you

Because you couldn't fly
    off the bridge
the balcony
    the buttressed vocation
of vying for protection
    you don't want
but need
    he can't help but
hit all the men
    hitting and hitting
on you
    a weight rests
a world rests
    on a sub(missive) plot line
spun through and past

the uninteresting
details
of your many rapes
he
the perfect hero
on his hero's journey
he
the perfect soldier
saving lives of
murderous men
but not himself
a murderer
he
running
because you
told him to
he
perfect
for the simple fact
he didn't rape you
a medal of honor
a fawn for his keeping

NOW SCREENING

BOY I AM | REAL BOY | TOMBOY | SHINJUKU BOYS |
BOYS DON'T CRY | A BOY NAMED SUE | SHE'S A BOY
I KNEW | LADYBOYS | BOY MEETS GIRL | IT'S A BOY
GIRL THING | I AM A GIRL | DRESSED AS A GIRL |
GIRL INSIDE | THE DANISH GIRL | SOLDIER'S GIRL |
DIFFERENT FOR GIRLS | A GIRL LIKE ME | GIRL | I AM
A WOMAN NOW | JUST LIKE A WOMAN | KISS OF THE
SPIDER WOMAN | LET ME DIE A WOMAN | WOMAN ON
FIRE | A FANTASTIC WOMAN | ANOTHER WOMAN |
MY DAD IS A WOMAN | NO ORDINARY MAN

HAVE IT YOUR WAY

Let's say I'm turned on by the ball pit. At Burger King,
we call it Play Palace. This the type of memory that shivers

tinsel when touched. I am encased in a glistening globe of
soft-boiled plastic. Dewed sweat dripping like flies. Behind me,

the nervous twitch of netting. Before me, a slide. The pit. The
children shrieking at the balls. The parents.

I am safe on my perch. Poised for a sensual descent. I must
permit myself this pleasure. I've had a hard day being a child.

The pit. The parents. I watch them watching. Children from
the waste up. There is something to this. A strategy, yes. For all

I know, their genitals are plastic, smooth like baby doll. Like
the balls glittered in spit. Bleach-fume oblivion, a hot breath

out the mouth of the slide, beckoning. I take a last look
through the porthole. The chaos of children who snuck fries

into the pit. Greased pagans slinging spheres of primary color.
Creation. It's Christmas Eve.

To me, the other children are also some sort of Jew-ish. To me,
Jew-ish means we are uninteresting and elsewhere.

Who else would be here, on this day, in this
shimmer of moment, between things. My people. The palace.

The parents are the Christians and their crotches. Curious
that there is something rather than nothing. That all of these

children were made for what. For their upper halves. Their
mouths. For what goes in them. In.

Are they really having it their way. For these are the sites in
which we are taught choice. I slide.

Friction tickles out a suggestion of body hair. Pursuing my
fullest pleasure, I lick the plastic interior. My tongue

crackles, bubble wrap. I'm safe. Swallowed. Forget form. The
words I'm held to. The prismatic light growing, an arachnid

forcefield spindling into my groin. I land. The sticky pit slow,
infuse me into its sugar-sweat and oils. Pleasure when I feel

nothing. Void is sensation. I want to slip a ball into my panties.
So I do. Have it my way. The smooth fupa of a Ken doll. Or

fuck it, why not Barbie, if I push in. Come on Barbie, let's go
party. Pop. Pleasure. My momentary shiver cut short by shouts.

Children's shouts. Then the parents. Because it's me. And so
I am told to split, meaning, to go elsewhere. To get out. Out.

SHE WANTED ME

for Grandma Gray

In the sentence "She's no longer
suffering," to what, to whom does she refer?
- Roland Barthes

Her name was gray and I liked it
timeless and practical it is often
associated with loss or neutral I was
not scared to lose her I was not able
to take her neutral name thus
forcing my father to call me by his
dead mother how cold   her name
was gray it is like a mystery of black
pavement poured concrete on her
body sinking she was an active
drowner clutching to life clutching
to me would she call me by my
dead name or   dad's name from
her grave   I scream in the night
because it's her

or was it ashes   gray like a thing
that twirls and sticks on the tongue
a flake of skin that's burnt into
nobody's memory my memory is
tied to her finger   twirling and
sinking we were both

abused a child   a grandparent is a
boring thing to lose I was not
scared to lose her a mother to
something she was always losing
track of children my father my
family's legacy was to lose sight of
what children are   what are they if
not something   you can't touch

abused as a child is a boring thing
to say they want details she was
gray and a matter of fact she would
tell me her details and ask was I
touched   she asked when I chose
to be fat

she was gray like the water drained
from a sink with a baby we all
chose to throw out her name gray
like a flock of letters in wind and
it's me who should catch them it's
me who should hear what she
wanted to say what she wanted
remembered was maybe a matter of
vengeance a drowning   a scream
in the night.

IF ANGELS

for Grandma Gertrude

Your God made me gay and I think
you can see that now from how
you hold me old in dreams after I
save you from Grandpa.

It said Dignity on your funeral
napkins and the Kentucky-men
wiped meatballs off their lips while
they stared at my hairstyle.

Your priest said he never knows
how women can sew and that you
"liked them adult coloring books
and crosswords." He said, "Yeah,
she could read."

Coloring books.   They talked
about adult coloring books at your
funeral.   They put a husband and
hobby in a tin can and rattled it off
the back of a hearse. Just morgued.

Two Kentucky-men tell me to sit
between them, their faces penny- dull
and looking. You'd have noticed.

Your marriage still belongs to Him.
Not even death a divorce.

You— trapped in the lines. I
bought you every color of pencil
God made.

I have violent sex on the peach
puffed quilt you made. I hope
you're not watching over me. But
maybe who cares if you're looking
down. Maybe the dead only see
clouds of energy. "Oh, she's feeling
very good right now," you'd think.
I mean feel.

No one expects me to be the kind
of person to write about grandmas.
Despite what bibles may say, I am
capable of being boring.
Crosswords in the morning. We
knew different words. Together.

You told me it doesn't make sense
that I'm going to Hell. You melted
sugar cubes on your tongue and
watched me read Harry Potter.

We did women's work together and talked women's talk. People forget I've done women's work. And I've talked. You said, "I've been believing men my whole life." And it made you mad. I listened.

Your daughter tells the Kentucky-men the story of a prank: After you, in preparation for me, bought out the world of its pink, she stole an obstetrician pad and wrote, "Made a mistake, this here is a baby boy." She told the story and laughed like the real joke wasn't there. Like she hadn't cast my curse.

I bought every color for you.

LEAVE HER ALONE

And now what.
I'm stuck on a carousel
seemingly in pursuit of a
young child humping her horse.

These things never end well.
Behind me, the aristocracy
in their carriage, cementing
blame on my back.

Beside me, a gray man
on a fixed horse in pursuit
of nothing. Blameless
with his withered balls.

I think he's about to die.
I think this carousel will stop
and the man will die and the
child will quit humping and

now what. We are told
the carousel song is called
Me and My Shadow. Indeed,
the light on my back casts.

Everyone is chasing a high
or a low, a shadow, a small
death. Me. Bobbing on bare
back, the eyeline of every father

shifting. Nervous the child
reveals too much. Hissing her
off the horse. She stumbles
to the outer decadence

of the karmic wheel. Something
to suck on awaits her if she holds
still for the camera. The song ends.
A mother whisks the child away

from me, no doubt, clearly
chasing her. Clearly short-circuiting
the fathers with my frenetic crotch.
I am too old to be alone. Or not old

enough. Blameless. The man
dies and now what.

[A BECKONING]

a place...

        ...away from here   far far
            ...a life lived
    lived...
         ...once
      lived

a place

      a prince   a price...
     ...all she ever wanted
   the tower...
        ...tuck

                 ... it's over
     ...tuck   and cover...
she's trapped...
       shhh shhh...
      ...a shore
   she...
a distant   ...should
   ...what price   a prince...
  a light....
     the tower...
   ...goodnight over there
moon...
    ...man
night...   ....light
    ....it's morning...

you find your bed made wet by a single worm.

the chirp of a bird waking up to bind you.

BAMBI IS DEAD BY NOW

And the blood is now baked on my father's headlights.
From within the steamy terror of the Toyota pickup, we watch
the doe twitching on the brightly lit road. My father shrugs.
He says, Animals simply shake off trauma. They shiver

their bodies and Poof. All better, he says. Something I should
consider. Get up, Bambi, says the Prince of the Woods,
a strange name for Daddy. Get up. Mother is dead.
All of the mothers are gone in this magic kingdom. This

fabled forest. This movie, it's all about gender. The owl warns of life,
puberty, and the pursuit of pussy to replace our dead,
our mothers are out of the way so boys can
get up. And get up. And get up, Bambi.

We need to keep cycling. Chase tails. Wheel
through feelings like death, the evil deeds of dogs and
men. Pick up where this carcass left. Don't worry,
my father says. He shook it off. But I saw.

She's a doe, not a deer. And she's dead. She's always dead.
So now where do I learn women of which the owl warns?
If my forest must hold men.

THE EARLY SEEDS IN SCENE

enters on a woman. version of a woman.
purse-clutched vision on a platform. transit.
voyeurs pass in briefcase-scurry. second-taked,
her billboard shouts   bold   for   being.
scene enters
on a woman trapped in the long stare of life. she is sacrifice.
dramatic.
she's a dream.

she dreams herself dead
on the floor of anybody's. not so much a floor
as a landing.   perhaps there. right there. where
standing. version of a woman. drifting. on a
platform. transit.
robbed of her clutch. men
looming over. is it over now. men
narrating her death. noticing
her body. naming
what large hands.   what strong arms.   what jaw line drawn
a
picture of something compelling.
what version of shame is under the
fig leaf they are lifting.
she is lying
still   pretty.   soul   sneaking   like   a
panty flash.
she could die for
that. she's dead.

all the better to see.
standing there she dreams
    juicing red across her lips to be
        noticed and more so unnoticed. she dreams
inverted   flowers these figs
      belonging to the only tree cursed because
                god hates them existing like that
god hates figs
    and she hates him back.

she dreams herself dead
    on a floor that is a beige carpet mundanely absorbing her. her
      flower folds inwards. it, in turn, absorbs the wasp that
stung it into life.
    it too is a part of her. this too
      is a part of her dream. she notices the carpet is covered
                    in stairs.
she is standing there and someone is noticing.
    this someone is reading but not reading a magazine.
      this someone is reading but not reading versions of
    women they could be. this.
    they have seen versions of this woman before.
      noticed-unnoticed like the flash of a billboard.
they too have seen her deaths.
    victim. villain. police station wallpaper.
this someone is feeling their own skin. it
    skin crawls. it skin lifts off its body to float the plat
                    form.
        its legs dangle and elongate.
      a spectral body hunched with intent.
        the haunt of a wasp approaching.

STEALTH NARCISSUS

for trancestors

Dead, you are my creatures.
Income elegy. I save you. I point

at the who-saved-who picture frame
sits empty, a pane of glass, a pool of water,

only water keeps us apart, my love,
myself. I am myself the boy I see.

The popular pronoun is now object
me. I, the abyss I'll never see

in this fountain dead, this glass empty,
this present where I portend my echo

to be you. Save me! You
gazing at myself as I'm dead.

Eros of erosion. The future has begun
its stiletto on cobblestone escape. You

gaze at myself like a fresh cut.
Fetch a fair price at market. I am

your bankable version.

I burn love in verse
for me, drown me for relief,
for a single kiss with what abyss.

With what abyss. Am I missing
everything, not to mention the point.

IT'S OUR PROBLEM FREE

I look into the eyes of a lover's lion tattoo
the locks of hair like yellow crayon
scrunching moles into waxy skin   appearance of a cub turned man

I look into its eyes to find meaning—   nothing

but no?   was looking in wrong place   tracing lines of hair   I see
a message   scribed in gilded strands

"hakuna matata"

Oh   I say   *Is that Swahili?*

It's Lion King   they say

Yup   *got* that *but*   *I think it might also be...*   *Swahili*

they are upset   I see   we are white   they say   *It means no worries*

Yup   *got* that *too...*

I take three seconds to Google the language of the tattoo they've had
for three years   indeed   Swahili   it means no worries

they flip over   (we're in bed)   tensing their calves   upon which another
moth-eaten ink   expressly gay   a scene wriggling out beneath
nonbinary leg hair   the characters:
music notes   a flat blue butterfly   both lifelessly hovering over

gid rainbow
hey say   *Don't worry   It's not what you think*   *This one's about Grandma*

try to remember   what it is they thought I was thinking
ut we touch skin to skin and ~no worries~

his person has been queer long before me
hey are perfectly gender neutral
s if a man and a woman had a baby
his person's partner has my same name and same birthday
his person has read More Than Two]

ue to Disney Dyke theme
hey say they just learned the term   "Pillow Princess"
hey describe: catatonic sleep-themed sex
y fingers flinch towards corrective Googling
et instead I nod: Snow— got it. White— of course.
leeping— check. They are Beauty— okay.

m I worried?   no   nothing in my   vapid blonde brain   my   helmet
ead
all me Smith   call me Scar   either way   I'll gladly pretend you're
nd of dead

this is queer sex—
nder like blue butterfly flapping flimsy against rigid rainbow
fuck them   rigid and royal   to the music of two flat notes

ee boop bee boop   I don't think I make them cum

47

TUNA IS A SYNONYM FOR MASCULINE

I don't want to prove how I got here.
I'd buy a t-shirt at the pride parade: Molested This Way.
Go ahead and she me. I'm a gay man.
I am the incognito tab of one boy, two butts.
I am poison-Mercury, as in Hermes is my daddy.
If you are trying to breed then don't bother to eat me.
And I am tired of women thinking I fancy them worms.
I am tired of direction and of streaming towards Him.
I suppose masculine is a synonym for tuna as well.

ME PROBLEM

Well, that was a negative sexual experience.
Had sex with a person who said they were non-binary
but was shocked to discover my tiny penis.

I spoon my trans friends for comfort and
have an idea! Let's all give each other tattoos.
They'll say t4t, except, I propose,
we get two tea bags tangled...code.

Not days after t4t branding my skin,
I promptly have sex with
an openly cis-identifying woman—
a first for me, if you can believe.
Something in me still scared
to be gay and okay in my
~cute~ new masculinity.

She kisses me at midnight.
It's New Years and I hardly know her.

Someone tries calling at midnight and that someone is dying.
I don't pick up.

New year new me.

She asks if I got a car to fuck in.
I offer a house and she scratches
the back of my head
the whole way home.
Her long nails with the gay ones cut
short is hot. I'd do it too,
but apparently, I need all of them.
Working my way in,
about to ask consent to be fisting.
She beats me to it.
She unbuckles my Fitbit.
She slings it off.
She fucking threw it.
She fucking threw my Fitbit.
Have to wait until the next morning
alarm goes off
to find it
she says,
"I don't want that in me."

I have no way to track
how long I didn't sleep.
Perhaps worried
I dream of only loving cis women.
Perhaps worried
I came in someone's tits.
First time for me.
This time my tiny penis
the one in shock.

Just because someone's femme
doesn't mean I have to be butch to it.
That's a me problem.
She's deeply gay and I like it.

She talks about another poet writing poetry about her.
I tell her I probably won't.

STATE OF UNDRESS

Yet another ghost leaks from a pussy and passes me by.
   Hardly a glance in my direction, scarcely a thank you.

A swing slips down from the ceiling, the ghost mounts
   and sways over its mother's heaving form, its toes

dipping in the warm ripples of her wet,
   the same wet that nearly drowned me.

To be clear, it's a shame I didn't drown.
   Tonight, only one ghost will glitter this room.

I remain the gentleman in the top hat,
   kneeling to help the starlet descend from her high.

This moment is not my moment.
   I defer to the woman whose queer virginity just sighed,

passing through to the next realm.
   We watch the train of its star-dusted gown shimmer off.

"I think I am no longer
   interested in certain dresses," my darling reflects.

Her eyes mist with the memory
   of some latter-day cabaret come to pass. I nod,

my recognition a corsage
       stuck to her syruped bloom. Her moment. Her shine.

"Yes," I avow. "I too
       only like certain dresses. Mostly the ones pressed tight

and dark." Her milk saucer eyes offer themselves. An unblemished
       pity in her ask. "As in the dresses you like seeing on
women?"

AND AS YOU SWEEP THE ROOM

Imagine the broom is someone you love
even if its handle gets rough   and whistle
You're a cruel queen   No one can hurt

you   Sweep the room   Taught to
whistle while we work angles   A strangled smile
for good people who need to see you seeing them

smiling   The kind of pleasant death they want for you They mean
peasant   get your knees on   You'll need them crawling out

from under that ancient rug   Dirt girl   You
not horny enough   And that apple you didn't offer
they're biting the shape of your throat   You were asking not for but to be it

A broom flipped to imaginary woman You dance her   She hits you
back and love They're all looking now You   looking plain in your glass
coffin

So visible   So what

BISEXUAL SNACK TIME

I guess I'm here again. Stomaching the streaks of bleach from past attempts
on this long stretch of laminate lunch top, looking for looks
        if not love— but from who.

Well, I'll tell you— from people who share my gender and... people who
don't. What a choice. What an interesting potential. Apple
orange. Tangerine. What a wild polarity— me and them— worth noting.
        To be fruit-cupped in a pedestrian menageric of sap.

I've been tense— ever since 2014 when a man sued Dole, panicked
to find preservatives, acid in his advertised as all-natural fruit. Man,
that's gotta sting. As far as looks go,
        it is true we stay young not forever but longer.

Which is why I am here. Again at the table, with a new and engorged
lunch box. Do you like it. Bench slide from the stench of banana breath
        and I'll tell you we're not friends. Fuck,

it's snack time. I've always hated this concept of time. Teacher,
don't you tell me when to carrot. Don't you tell me when I want
        a measured treat. So tense

from the contents of a zip-locked asphyxiation. I want
to use the napkin I saved to wipe sweat from your
        carefully cut choices. Me or them.

Ice breaker: Do you prefer certain genitals over others. And why. Why do you think that is. Because I think
that's what we're talking about. After you copy the homework
that I copied first, so now

you want a taste. You want to share my snack, my time, and it's fine. I blame the overarching context of cafeteria.
The lunch lady who never asked to be named.

I'M A PROBLEM AGAIN

Outside the food store,
    a man asks,
    "Are you a princess or a pea— nis!"
So the story goes.

    The prince needs to find a real princess,
real because she's pained
    and purpled
by the slightest discomfort.

    A nearby woman is shocked to witness.
"Horrible," she says to me.
"I'm very disturbed."

Look at her. Looking
    at me. I will later find her in the parking lot
and slash her bag of frozen carrots.

Oh, how I long to be pea.

I FAKE IT SO REAL I AM BEYOND

more than bedded
        less than bathed
I am beyond bodied

        finally

my cake cut for nobody
        no body cut for me
I used to insist
        on proof

is this real
        am I

but now
        I can't care
as long as we commit to the bit
        the contract made of cake
put your name on it
        sign here to submit and
we promise

you don't have to be a man
        you can
be a woman-plus and
        join us
you'll be the girl with the most

...SOUND SEARCH...

It's music to you here
    I dream the seaweed
always greener In
    somebody else
my mistake
    Perhaps it's better
down where it's wetter...
    Perhaps we're in luck
down here We are devoted
    to floating full time
We are happy
    as after the waves
we roll What more
    am I looking
      ...

[AN UNBECKONING]

Lead me to the one
who loves
        Gleaming
    in the skies Goodnight
little star   Where dreams
        really do
come Where dreams
really do When you
    leave the world
Good-
    bye
D u s t
    It's that easy
We're rising off t
        he floor.
At last we have a mother
What pleasure
    Make us pockets
        and sing
    Story come
        to an end
        I'll never be
the lost
boy You make me
Complete
me as Mother I
  am not It seems
the victory is mine

THE DAY I KNEW

for Baby

Because it took me so long
to realize that words like song
    are something.
Though not greater than flesh.
Though not more captivating than
    the bitter breeze that brought me.
How to let it in slow. I thought
window. I thought
    how does it feel,
because the bend
in the gorge moved fast
    that day. Men
aligning the tips of their dicks
with the current
    because it feels good.
They say,
do what feels. Because
    my bra, which they say
I am wearing for sport
is wet against numb and inverted nipples,
    turning in to an emotion,
because it's time and tired,
because my friend who I named Baby
    who named me Baby too
tells me something in the gorge that day,

tells me, Baby, cis people don't spend all
    their time thinking about this.
Oh. So it's that simple.
Because the vultures in the pine trees
    won't fix their posture either,
won't stop staring at my tits.
And the word feels good.
    The choice to speak it is great.
Down in the gorge
an echo.

AM I STILL A BROKEN TILE

Sisters. What whispers have you? Circle secrets. Candle to the chin. Woman-shaped shadows walk the lawn. They call it gossip, what we do. Windchime warnings, as they haunt the parameters of our picket fence. Our picket, performing the chore of protection. Our fence, a slight string of sighs, insinuations. A flutter of freckled moths forms a mosaic against our window, shields us from their gaze, carries whispers to the wind, searching for other fences and flames with which to kill ourselves, over and covert again. Bitch hunt. They call it complaint. We become the trouble by invoking its name. They tell us we are poison and therefore vaccine. Drain milk from our bodies. Dig graves in our lawn. They call it lies. Hysteria. Throw dirt on the herstory, Freud's flaccid exposure, they were touched by Daddy after all. Funny. How they want to hear the names we whisper, never those we shout. Our fence, the whites of averted eyes. The mosaic is a picture of our tits.

THE COST OF ACTING

The French, Dutch and Russian puppets
who have cut their strings for you
lie limp on the bed.
Wooden breasts carved
in continual heave.
So now you get to breathe.

Was it worth it? Real boy.

...THROUGH MAGNETIC MYLAR LOOPS...

There you see her
    She doesn't have a lot
to say Floating
    in the blue
You've got the mood
    prepared
Now is your moment
    She won't say a word
You want to kiss her Don't
    try to hide You are dying
to try Do what
    the music says
It's possible
    she wants you too
...

IT'S A BEAUTIFUL DAY

won't you be my neighbor

this beauty wood
this cosmic weave
this loom loom loom

shadow-glue on the doorstep
shit-stain on the sheets
corse flecks of pity rain
they all saw the body leave

shutter-creeped
wilt-necked
the tulips dripped
early

good morning
could you be mine
would you
I searched for eyes behind

I always wanted
to be a neighbor
just like you

IT WAS THE SAME I THROUGHOUT

Yes, I have committed.
Sexed and solitary in my mutant cell,
watch me scratch sins on porcelain forest-green

imported from classrooms long gone,
chalk dust deviling somewhere, the rainbow,
the chalk reads, *I will tell no lies.* Why,

oh why can't I speak no weakness if not when spoken
to, if not when told to be good, I am older now, over
that rainbow stretched away, I reach over

straining through its spectrum
like a body breaks to build.
Watch me un-tomb her,

dragged up the tower steps by what hair she has left.
I pretend to love her with a tortoiseshell comb. *Little Jenny.*
You were bad as I am, I am as you already

were, I whisper. *You are not my lawfully wedded life.*
You are not my picket white. I stand with her no longer.
I hand over the chalk, her bones

cracking with their grip. *Take it.*
She will tell no lies, she will not
be distanced from her muted crimes

and you. You will watch, as I do, as I make her scratch my sins
for what public viewing speaks of private parts,
you, owed proof of what we're made, you

absolve her as if she were not I, how could I.
How could I commit. I am the baron of our body.
You wished to save her from my kiss.

...THE CHOICE IS REAL.

Make your choice
    But without voice
how can I
    On land it's preferred for
ladies not to say
    a word Don't
underestimate
    the importance of body
Some
    couldn't pay the price
And do I help them
    I admit in the past
Seen light
    Made a switch
All my ways
    I've mended I'm afraid
I had to
    'Cross
the coals The bridge
    its toll Those
unfortunate souls *La voce*
    to me Now sing
The only way
    to what you want
is to become
    human
        yourself.

ASTROTURF

And I'm no longer finished
This grief screeching
    tire smoke
peels back to your memory
    Feeling petty on a Sunday
gods and games aside
    Just because
you moved your sand
    castle skyward
doesn't mean I can't
    knock it down

Aries, I
tantrum your turf
    or I wish you were there
Trapped in that time
under your pine towers
    you took me
hands grazed my bare chest
    focus soft and
fixed on my grafts
    for the first time and this the
first time
    their bud-like nature occurred in
you
    You said
    they're beautiful

Ask Leo moon how many men
get to hear their nipple's praise
        from a mother no less, no
less a memory than a
        hole where I think you dug
It hurts me

Saturdays
I am alone as a child
        my bedroom a laboratory
of toys with as many types of genitals
        I was trying to grow things too
you know
        rearranging turf with what blocks and seeds
It seemed everything I made you deemed
        infertile

The turf you assumed natural, my love
there's no natural now
        any more than me
and you knew that
        it's not natural for me to say

                                        my love

and you knew
        that you knew
well

The turf you kept smells
like a child pissed
        and pissing itself

Something I like to think
you did for me an ode
    my condition a constant soil
I was only a girl
    who could blame and
growth wants that
    kind of death
but I know
    it's
your smell
your territory
your boxwooded turf
    a Taurus
No secret your garden was
    kept

All the earth a staged
indulgence
    you charcuteried elements
like fire
    and airs
your gem-clutched
    daylight is
the kind of blue to which you knew
    you would return
at the end of this passive
    something else waits
but I'm sorry it's
    nothing
you can keep

Blue hills were hills that I loved
They aren't mine but
    they felt it
when you took them
    your hooves dancing dirt clouds
my wincing skies
    blue like the place you knew
returning
In the end
that walk was all you ever wanted
    your turf swelled with every step
into me
    and that is
why I moved away

Our last walk
I tried stepping into you
    boot-laced and blundering
You gave me little
    some
you said
    I see myself returning
Your hill to

I hated that blue
but I believe you
    We women need
believe
    each other and I am one
a sort of

        woman
really

Do you
        or do I believe
that
        me
You've known me
You've seen me
        grace the halls of girldom
you came
        mid-damage I grew
faster
        something of a miracle
grow so as not to
        be your child

You've seen me and
wondered
        what woman was I learning
if not you If not
        the flowers you tossed
I didn't catch
        If not your drift
then whose dream
You wondered
what parasitic graft was this
        small bud grifting off of
other small buds budding
        heads but

together. Girls

    I learned from
and to be Though
    women
I never thought to become one but
    I can say I have learned to love
moreso the type of women you
    call men Moreso
you
    in the end And
versions of women
    vying
my attention
    peaked on
in the shape of
    it

I think what it is
is learning to love
    that child
and I'm some kind of infertile
    you know
my child will only ever be me
    and if girl doesn't exist then
I was one
    and I've learned to love
her so
    she's sealed
I won't allow her the

kind of death
        for growth
you know
        I won't let her woman-
hood but that
        doesn't suggest I
somehow let her go

The turf you keep
        toiling
in this late
        a climate of categorical
these beds raised beyond anything
        you've grown and died for
The turf you
        kept
missing
        those hands
they graze for something
        like love but
in order
        to love why would they need
to understand
I think it's that
we've done a bad job
        honoring
seeing
        you honoring anything old
I know vintage more
        than elder

I know nothing of
        how you suffered
except the pains of which
        I've suffered more

Staggering
how much vintage is now
        plastic
the plastics that killed you
        you relate to me
as if your mammary-maims proved
        more provincial
but I understand
        Bold of us to assume
we understood you
        How many ways were we happy
to bury
        forgetting
dirt is often
        fertile

There is a star named
after you
        this because money
a certificate
        I knocked off its plastic
stand last Saturday
        Sunday
I believed
        this week

I am no longer
    finished
They bought you a
    plot in the eye of
Taurus
    I don't look
for it
    hoping it won't look
to me
    won't call me
beautiful
    how stars creep
in daylight blue
    invisible
the place you knew

NOTES & ACKNOWLEDGEMENTS

"The choice is real" is a line from Jack Spicer's poem "IX" in *Billy the Kid* (Enkidu Surrogate, 1958).

The epigraph is borrowed from *We Both Laughed In Pleasure: The Selected Diaries of Lou Sullivan* (Nightboat Books, 2019).

"Tangled the ribbon of my favorite VHS...," "...attempt the untangle...," "...sound search...," "...through magnetic mylar loops...," and "...the choice is real." are all found language poems from Disney's *The Little Mermaid* (1989).

"And fell through the dark" pulls language from *In the Night Kitchen* by Maurice Sendak (Harper and Row, 1970).

"And as you sweep the room" references language from Disney's *Snow White* (1938).

"Things I have time" is inspired by Bhanu Kapil's "Twelve Questions" (*The Vertical Interrogation of Strangers* (Kelsey Street Press, 2001).

"It's a beautiful day" references language from *Mr. Rogers' Neighborhood* (1968–2001) and was written the day my stepmother, Diane, passed.

"Now screening" is a found language poem made up of film titles. All of the films are about trans people.

"I fake it so real I am beyond" references language from Hole's song, "Doll Parts" (DGC Records, *Live Through This*, 1994).

"It was the same I throughout" references the confessions of Saint Augustine.

"[an unbeckoning]" references language from Disney's *Peter Pan* (1953).

Thank you to the editors of the presses and journals in which these poems (often previous versions) first appeared:

o•blk editions for publishing previous versions of these poems in the chapbook, *Astroturf*.

Mundus Press: "And fell through the dark," "[a beckoning]," and "[an unbeckoning]"

Hot Pink: "Bisexual snack time"

Boulevard: "The choice is real"

Black Warrior Review: "Stealth narcissus"

Nightboat Books: "Me problem" in *We Want It All: An Anthology of Radical Trans Poetics*

b l u s h lit: "It's our problem free"

Metatron Press: "Tonight I'm a problem"

The New Guard: "If angels"

My gratitude to the folks at Metatron Press for handling my work with such care—Ashley Obscura and Hannah Karpinski, you were both amazing to work with. Thank you to Fariha Róisín for selecting me for the 2022 Metatron Press Prize for Rising Authors and for composing such beautiful thoughts about my work.

Forever and ever grateful to Peter Gizzi, Ocean Vuong, Cameron Awkward-Rich, and CAConrad for your support and guidance.

My whole heart to Ace for your perpetual encouragement, sharp eyes, and ceaseless love. A million lifetimes of thanks to Ellis for raising me into the poet I am today. A big wet kiss to Elle for hyping me to the moon. Love you forever, Anto, for watching me grow all these years and supporting my merman dreams. Caroline and Rachelle— G.B.A. forever.

I could not have done this without my community and friends: DK, Samson, Cyrus, Ailbhe, Baby, Al, Vick, Jina, Dshaun, Nellie, Juliana, Jon, Zoe, Tommi, Brendan, Mitra, Chloe, Julien, Mattia and the many others who've put wind beneath my little poetry wings. Thank you, Diane, for your love and bravery in the end.

JAYSON KEERY

Jayson Keery is based in Western Massachusetts, where they completed their MFA in poetry at the University of Massachusetts Amherst. *The Choice Is Real* is their first full-length collection. They are the author of the chapbook *Astroturf* (o·blēk editions, edited by Peter Gizzi, 2022). Their work has appeared in Boulevard, Black Warrior Review, Hot Pink, b l u s h lit, Peach Mag, and others. They have been anthologized in Mundus Press's *Nocturnal Properties*, Nightboat Books' *We Want It All: An Anthology of Radical Trans Poetics*, and Pilot Press London's *A Queer Anthology of Rage*. They received the 2022 Metatron Press Prize for Rising Authors, selected by Fariha Róisín, and the 2021 Daniel and Merrily Glosband MFA Fellowship, selected by Wendy Xu. A complete list of publications, awards, and interviews live online at JaysonKeery.com.